Lexcel Risk Management Toolkit

Related titles from Law Society Publishing:

Lexcel Business Continuity Planning Toolkit
The Law Society

Lexcel Client Care Toolkit (2nd edn)
The Law Society

Lexcel Financial Management and Business Planning Toolkit
The Law Society

Lexcel Information Management Toolkit
The Law Society

Lexcel People Management Toolkit
The Law Society

All books from Law Society Publishing can be ordered through good bookshops or direct from our distributors, Prolog, by telephone 0870 850 1422 or e-mail **lawsociety@prolog.uk.com**. Please confirm the price before ordering.

For further information or a catalogue, please contact our editorial and marketing office by e-mail **publishing@lawsociety.org.uk**.

Lexcel Risk Management Toolkit

The Law Society

The Law Society

ISBN 978-1-85328-912-5

Published in 2011 by the Law Society
113 Chancery Lane, London WC2A 1PL

Typeset by Columns Design XML Ltd, Reading
Printed by Hobbs the Printers, Ltd, Totton, Hants

The paper used for the text pages of this book is FSC®certified. FSC (the Forest Stewardship Council®) is an international network to promote responsible management of the world's forests.

Contents

Preface

Effective risk management is a fundamental requirement in running a successful legal practice. It is particularly important when organisations operate in a regulated sector and in a challenging and changing economic environment.

Poor risk management will almost inevitably lead to undesirable consequences such as errors, complaints and claims. It could eventually lead to more serious consequences such as prosecution, reputational damage or the closing down of a business. However, logic dictates that the obverse is equally true. Effective risk management will lead to outcomes such as:

- compliance with regulatory requirements;
- efficient case management procedures;
- high quality client care and service provision;
- increased client retention;
- reduced numbers of complaints and claims;
- reduced insurance premiums;
- an enhanced reputation.

The *Lexcel Risk Management Toolkit* is designed to help practices achieve sustained high levels of performance in areas such as client care as well as providing guidance on meeting the requirements of the Lexcel standard. Whereas the Toolkit outlines some of the theory behind risk management, the emphasis is on covering the practicalities in the context of a legal practice. To this end, the Toolkit includes:

- specific examples of strategic, operational and regulatory risks;
- specific examples of how risks can be treated and monitored;
- guidance on recognised risk management methodologies such as SWOT analyses and risk mapping.

The Toolkit also includes a wide range of template documents and aide mémoires including:

- a risk management policy;
- a risk register;
- a risk referral form;
- an operational risk flowchart;
- a file review checklist;
- a strategic risk review agenda;
- role definitions.

We hope that you will find the *Lexcel Risk Management Toolkit* useful both as a reference guide and as a practical resource in your day-to-day work.

The Lexcel Office would like to thank John O'Sullivan of BCL Knowledge for his contribution to this Toolkit.

Lexcel Office
The Law Society

1 The risk management framework

1.1 Overview

A risk management framework is the term used to describe the structure of, and approach to, risk management in an organisation. A risk management framework should:

- be an integral part of strategic planning and review;
- focus on both process and culture;
- include a clearly defined policy;
- embrace the whole organisation.

An overview of a risk management framework is illustrated in **Figure 1.1**.

1.2 Strategic planning

1.2.1 Context

Risk management should not be viewed in isolation. It must be looked at in the context of everything a practice does, in particular, its strategic aims and objectives. In order to position the importance of risk management, the fundamental question

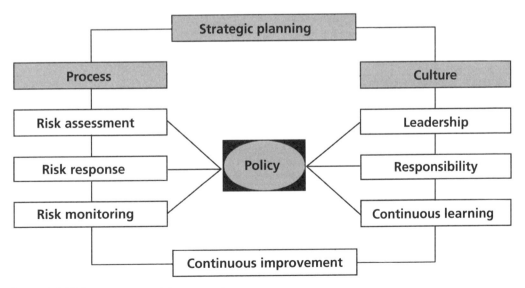

Figure 1.1 Risk management framework

practices should ask is: 'What are the events that could prevent us from achieving our objectives?'

The answers to that question will undoubtedly provide a compelling case for ensuring that risk management is an integral part of strategic planning. Deployed effectively, risk management is an enabler that supports the achievement of aims and objectives such as:

- running a profitable business (private practices);
- delivering cost-effective services (in-house departments);
- providing high quality legal advice;
- providing high levels of client service;
- complying with regulatory and legislative requirements.

1.2.2   Key performance indicators

Key performance indicators or KPIs are the measures against which performance can be gauged, either quantitatively or qualitatively. In a legal practice, typical KPIs include fee income, profit and client satisfaction. Once identified, KPIs can then form the basis for defining a practice's business objectives.

For example:

- Achieve an increase in fee income of x%
- Achieve a gross profit of £y
- Achieve an average client satisfaction rating of 96%

The Lexcel standard includes a range of KPIs that are explicitly aligned to risk management, namely, indemnity insurance claims, client complaints and file review data. In order to optimise the benefits of risk management it is recommended that these risk KPIs are utilised to set improvement objectives.

For example:

- Achieve zero indemnity insurance claims
- Reduce justified client complaints by x%
- Achieve a file review compliance average of 95%

It is good practice to include risk-related objectives within a business plan as this provides a focus for improvement and reflects the level of its importance.

1.3   The risk management process

In essence, there are three key stages within the risk management process:

- Stage 1: the identification and evaluation of risks
- Stage 2: the control or treatment of risks
- Stage 3: the monitoring and reporting of risks

Further detailed information on each of the above is contained in **Chapters 3, 4** and 5 respectively.

1.4 Risk management policy

A practice's overarching principles and guidelines relating to risk management must be set out in a policy document and communicated to all people within its scope. An effective risk management policy should quickly convey a series of key elements to the reader, namely:

* Commitment
* Scope
* Approach
* Responsibilities
* Review

A suggested template for a risk management policy can be found at **Annex 1A**.

1.5 Risk management culture

For risk management to be sustained and consistent, it should be embedded within the culture of your practice. In essence, this means things like:

* senior managers leading by example;
* all employees understanding their responsibility for identifying, managing and reporting risks;
* effective communication of risk priorities and risk performance;
* continuous learning aimed at ensuring that people at all levels have the competence to manage risk.

Further detailed information on each of the above is contained in **Chapter 6**.

1.6 Continuous improvement

Practices should seek to continually improve both risk management processes and risk management culture. Improvements can be generated in the following ways:

* by setting targets using a risk management action plan;
* via risk monitoring and strategic reviews;
* by encouraging staff to suggest improvements;
* through analysis of risk data;
* by acting on feedback from external sources such as Lexcel assessors, the Solicitors Regulation Authority (SRA) and insurers;
* by benchmarking performance against other practices.

In terms of underlying philosophy, it is best to judge risk management in terms of compliance and performance improvement. For example, consider the benefits of meeting the client care requirements in terms of compliance and delivering consistently high levels of client service.

If risk management is hindering the achievement of your aims and objectives, it is not working and your approach will need to be re-designed.

Annex 1A
Risk management policy

Commitment

[*Name of practice*] is committed to sound corporate governance and has made risk management an integral part of its strategic planning and review processes. Risk management will be highlighted in induction and will underpin all practice management procedures.

Scope

The scope of this policy embraces all permanent and temporary employees, and systems or processes for the identification, control and monitoring of risks. The Lexcel standard requires that the following categories of risk be included:

- Strategic risk
- Operational risk
- Regulatory risk

Approach

The practice has initiated a systematic approach to the management of risk including:

- ensuring that the office manual is fully compliant with the Lexcel standard;
- compiling a risk register;
- compiling a risk management action plan;
- maintaining a list of work that the practice will and will not undertake;
- conducting an annual review of complaints data;
- providing staff briefing and training on risk identification, control and reporting.

Responsibilities

Risk Manager

The designated Risk Manager for the practice is [*employee name*]. He/she has overall responsibility for risk management in the practice.

Senior management team

The senior management team is responsible for determining the strategic direction of the practice and for carrying out strategic risk reviews. It is also responsible for creating the culture and environment for risk management to operate effectively throughout the practice.

Supervisors

Supervisors have primary responsibility for managing risk on a day-to-day basis. They are also responsible for promoting risk awareness within their teams.

Staff

All staff have a responsibility for identifying, controlling and reporting risk at a level appropriate to their role. In order to facilitate this, all staff are required to keep up to date with the procedures outlined in the office manual.

Review

In order to ensure that it remains fit for purpose, this policy will be formally reviewed at least annually by the senior management team. This review process will also serve as a means of continually improving the practice's approach to risk management.

Signed:

[*Name*], Risk Manager

Date:

2 Types of risk

2.1 Risk categories

Types of risks can vary within a law practice. We acknowledge this and base our categorisations on the Lexcel standard's three categories of risk:

- Strategic risk
- Operational risk
- Regulatory risk

Note: The above categories are not mutually exclusive, with some risks being relevant to more than one category. For example, risks relating to health and safety may be categorised as either operational or regulatory. Similarly, risks relating to legal sector reforms could be categorised as either strategic or regulatory. The important thing is that risks are identified – not how they are specifically categorised.

2.2 Strategic risk

Strategic risks are those events and consequences that could affect the viability or success of your practice. These types of risks are often triggered by external factors such as the economy or catastrophic events. Listed below are a number of typical strategic risk themes and examples of risks associated with those themes.

Theme	Associated risks
Business continuity	Lack of contingency planning for severe business interruption
	Inadequate insurance to cover a catastrophic event
Business strategy	Limited ability to identify sources of potential business due to absence of marketing strategy
	Over-reliance on a small number of clients or insufficient breadth of types of work
	Inflexible or high cost leases on premises
	Insufficient investment in new technology
Competition	Lack of awareness of fee structures and capabilities of other practices
Economy	Exposure to changes in interest rates
	Insufficient preparedness for a downturn in the economy
Finance	Lax systems on the control of expenditure and monitoring of cash flow
	Inaccurate and/or untimely billing

Theme	Associated risks
Governance	Lack of partnership agreement or members' agreement
	Lack of clear succession plan relating to future management and/or ownership of the practice
	Ineffective performance measurement and review
People	Shortage of skills and knowledge relevant to changing legal landscape
	Lack of planned approach to the recruitment and retention of employees

2.3 Operational risk

Operational risks are those events and consequences that arise as a result of carrying out day-to-day business activities. For example, a lack of consistent, rigorous procedures relating to the start, progress and conclusion of matters would expose your practice to the risk of complaints and indemnity claims.

It is worth noting that some operational risks can escalate into strategic risks if action is not taken to address them. For example, aside from any regulatory implications, continued inconsistent application of client care requirements could result in significant loss of business and compromise the viability of the practice.

Listed below are a number of typical operational risk themes and examples of risks associated with those themes.

Theme	Associated risks
Case management	Ineffective procedures for vetting new instructions
	Ineffective procedures for dealing with high risk matters
	Inconsistent application of professional rules
	Inconsistent approach to the recording and monitoring of key dates
	Inconsistent approach to the identification of conflicts of interests
	Ineffective procedures relating to undertakings
	Ineffective procedures for quality assuring barristers and other service providers
Clients	Lack of process for gauging client feedback
	Ineffective procedures for dealing with client complaints
Health and safety	An unsafe environment for staff, clients and other visitors to the practice
	Absence of a policy on working away from the office
	Inconsistent approach to staff induction
Information management	Insufficiently robust systems for safeguarding client confidentiality and other information assets of the practice
Information technology	Insufficient controls to identify inappropriate e-mails
	Insufficient controls to identify misuse of the Internet
People	Lack of clarity of responsibilities, accountabilities and reporting lines
	Inadequate processes for monitoring employee workloads and capability

2.4 Regulatory risk

Regulatory risks are those events and consequences that could arise as a result of changes in regulatory or legislative frameworks. They could also arise as a result of failure to adhere to current regulatory and legislative frameworks. Listed below are a number of typical regulatory risk themes and examples of risks associated with those themes.

Theme	Associated risks
Data protection	Failure to register with the Information Commissioner
	Lack of staff knowledge of the principles of the Data Protection Act 1998
Health and safety	Failure to carry out risk assessments and record the significant findings
	Lack of a competent person as defined under the Health and Safety at Work etc. Act 1974
Money laundering	Non-compliance with Money Laundering Regulations 2007
	Non-compliance with Proceeds of Crime Act 2002
	Non-compliance with Terrorism Act 2000
	Inconsistent approach to the verification of client identity
	Inconsistent approach to carrying out client due diligence
	Lack of staff knowledge of the relevant legislation
	Insufficient record keeping
People	Lack of effective policy on the avoidance of discrimination and the promotion of equality and diversity
Solicitors' Accounts Rules	Inconsistent adherence to the key principles
Solicitors' Code of Conduct	Breach of requirements of rules, especially rule 5

Note: The tables above are not intended to provide either a prescriptive or an exhaustive list of risks.

3 Risk assessment

3.1 Overview

There are two distinct elements within the risk assessment process, namely:

- identification of risks;
- evaluation of risks.

3.2 Risk identification

> **Note:** It is important here that you apply an approach that is suited to the type and size of your practice. For smaller practices with a narrow band of matter types it may be sufficient to identify risks through a simple brainstorming exercise. For larger practices, the risk identification process tends to be more complex when structured methodologies such as SWOT and PEST analyses are utilised. Further detailed information on SWOT and PEST analyses is contained in **Chapter 7**.

The first critical step is to establish the strategic, operational and regulatory risks faced by your practice. In many practices, formal risk identification takes place at least annually – ideally as part of the strategic planning process.

In addition to the above structured identification process, each employee should seek to identify risks on a continual basis. Typical processes through which risks can be identified include:

- file opening procedures;
- general supervision;
- matter or caseload reviews;
- file reviews.

3.3 Risk evaluation

The primary purpose of risk evaluation is to enable the level or severity of risks to be gauged. The evaluation of risk is usually based on both the likelihood of its occurrence and the impact of its consequences.

As part of the evaluation process it is good practice to rate levels of risk, for example, as high, medium or low. This allows informed decisions to be made on the urgency and the vigour with which risks need to treated.

Note: As with risk identification, the extent of risk evaluation could vary depending on the scale and complexity of the practice. For example, ratings could be arrived at through professional judgement and consensus based on your knowledge of your practice and the profession. Alternatively, practices may elect to use a more structured technique such as risk mapping. Further detailed information on risk mapping is contained in **Chapter 8.**

3.4 Risk register

It is good practice to record your risks on a risk register. Capturing information in this way has a number of advantages. For example, a risk register provides:

- a sharp focus on the highest risks facing your practice;
- a framework for grading your risks in order of severity;
- a sound basis for action planning, monitoring and review.

An example of a risk register can be found at **Annex 3A**. An alternative version, utilising a numerical risk rating system, can be found at **Annex 3B**.

Annex 3A
Risk register 1

Risk			Level		
Ranking	Event	Potential consequences	Likelihood	Impact	Rating
1	Ineffective performance measurement and management review processes	Non-compliance with Code of Conduct Skills and knowledge gaps Complaints Indemnity claims	High	High	High
2	Inconsistent application of procedure for verifying client identity	Fraudulent activity Exposure to disciplinary action and/or prosecution Reputational damage	High	High	High
3	Insufficiently robust systems relating to security of data	Breach of client confidentiality Complaints Indemnity claims Reputational damage	High	High	High
4	Lack of structured system for allocation of work	Excessive employee workload leading to errors Loss of key staff Complaints Indemnity claims	High	High	High
5	Insufficiently robust systems for vetting instructions	Complaints Indemnity claims Reputational damage	High	High	High
6	Non-compliance with health and safety legislation	Injury to staff and visitors Exposure to litigation Exposure to prosecution Reputational damage	High	High	High
7	Periodic instances of poor cash flow due to inconsistent approach to billing	Loss of income Bank charges and interest	High	Low	Medium

Risk			Level		
Ranking	Event	Potential consequences	Likelihood	Impact	Rating
8	Inconsistent compliance with Code of Conduct	Complaints Indemnity claims	Low	High	Medium
9	Insufficient flow of new instructions	Financial viability Staff redundancies	Low	High	Medium
10	Catastrophic event such as fire or flooding	Business interruption Loss of income Physical damage to premises	Low	High	Medium

Annex 3B
Risk register 2 (numerical rating)

Key

1–4 = Low risk
5–15 = Medium risk
16–36 = High risk

Risk			Level			
Ranking	Event	Potential consequences	Likelihood	Impact	Index	Rating
1	Ineffective performance measurement and management review processes	Non-compliance with rule 5 Skills and knowledge gaps Complaints Indemnity claims	6	6	36	High
2	Inconsistent application of procedure for verifying client identity	Fraudulent activity Exposure to disciplinary action and/or prosecution Reputational damage	5	6	30	High
3	Insufficiently robust systems relating to security of data	Breach of client confidentiality Complaints Indemnity claims Reputational damage	5	5	25	High
4	Lack of structured system for allocation of work	Excessive employee workload leading to errors Loss of key staff Complaints Indemnity claims	6	4	24	High
5	Insufficiently robust systems for vetting instructions	Complaints Indemnity claims Reputational damage	5	4	20	High

Risk			Level			
Ranking	Event	Potential consequences	Likelihood	Impact	Index	Rating
6	Non-compliance with health and safety legislation	Injury to staff and visitors Exposure to litigation Exposure to prosecution Reputational damage	4	4	16	High
7	Periodic instances of poor cash flow due to inconsistent approach to billing	Loss of income Bank charges and interest	5	3	15	Medium
8	Inconsistent compliance with rule 2	Complaints Indemnity claims	3	4	12	Medium
9	Insufficient flow of new instructions	Financial viability Staff redundancies	2	5	10	Medium
10	Catastrophic event such as fire or flooding	Business interruption Loss of income Physical damage to premises	1	6	6	Medium

4 Risk response

4.1 Overview

Once your risks have been identified and evaluated, the next key stage is to consider how they can be managed and controlled – this is known as risk response. There are four recognised approaches to the treatment of risks, namely:

- Tolerate
- Terminate
- Transfer
- Treat.

4.2 Tolerate

Some risks could be deemed to be acceptable to a practice. Generally this would occur either when a risk is rated as low or a risk has a potential 'upside'. An upside risk is usually an event that could provide an opportunity as well as a threat and, therefore, could be a risk worth taking.

For example, recruiting a business development manager would put an increase on overheads but could potentially lead to a significant increase in new instructions.

4.3 Terminate

This would involve not pursuing a particular course of action because the potential consequences are deemed to be undesirable.

Examples of risk avoidance could include:

- ceasing to carry out a particular type of work because it is not profitable;
- refusing to accept an instruction because there is insufficient expertise in the practice to deal with the matter effectively.

4.4 Transfer

In effect, this involves shifting the risk to, or sharing the risk with, another party.

Examples of risk transfer could include:

- taking out insurance cover to reduce the impact of a catastrophic event;
- taking out insurance cover to indemnify against claims;
- outsourcing areas of work or support services.

4.5 Treat

4.5.1 Likelihood and impact

As detailed earlier, there are two essential components to risk – likelihood and impact. It therefore follows that if you reduce either likelihood or impact (or both) you will reduce risk.

Examples of treating a risk could include:

- using anti-virus software to reduce the likelihood of damage to the integrity of IT systems;
- carrying out file reviews to reduce the impact of errors and omissions in case management.

When looking at treating risks it has to be acknowledged that it is not always possible to control the likelihood of some risks – this is especially true of strategic risk.

For example, adverse economic conditions or the occurrence of catastrophic events are outside your control. However, you can take steps to lessen the impact of these situations, such as:

- taking out fixed rate loans to hedge against hikes in interest rates;
- compiling a business continuity plan to reduce the impact of a catastrophic event.

In terms of volume, and indeed often severity, the majority of risks faced by legal practices are operational risks. The Lexcel standard contains a number of requirements that are designed specifically to mitigate these types of operational risks. These are as follows.

4.5.2 Supervision

Clear lines of supervisory responsibility and active ongoing supervision are an essential part of risk reduction. For example:

- Checks on correspondence will reduce the risk of supervisors being unaware of delays in the progress of matters or other sources of potential client dissatisfaction.
- Effective communication structures will reduce the risk of staff being unaware of priorities, policies and procedures.
- Matter reviews will reduce the risk of inaccurate or untimely billing and the provision of inappropriate legal advice.
- Direct supervisor involvement in the allocation of work will reduce the risk of matter handlers becoming overloaded or taking on matters that they do not have the capability to deal with.

4.5.3 Lists of work

Practices must define and list the types of work they will and will not undertake. This approach will reduce the risks of:

*   taking on work for which the practice has insufficient resources to tackle;
*   taking on work in which the practice has insufficient expertise.

The key to this risk reduction process is communication. All relevant staff must be made aware of the list of acceptable/unacceptable work – this could be a section in the office manual or a page on the Intranet. Moreover, all relevant staff must be informed in the event of any changes to the list.

4.5.4 Generic risks

Practices must maintain a list of generic risks by work type, particularly those that are the source of claims.

Examples could include:

*   failure to comply with time limits;
*   cases being handled at too low a level;
*   breach of undertakings.

It may also be appropriate to define and list high risk practice areas, for example, conveyancing, litigation and personal injury. In addition to defining lists, effective risk reduction practice here would include:

*   communication – as outlined in **4.5.3**;
*   supervision – especially allocation of work and monitoring of workloads;
*   file reviews (see **4.5.11**).

4.5.5 Managing instructions

The fact that instructions may be deemed high risk does not necessarily mean they should not be accepted.

For example, a matter may be well within the compass of the practice from a technical competence perspective. However, the potential loss in the event of a negligence claim might be at the upper end of maximum liability cover. If a decision is taken to proceed, the case management approach should reflect the higher risk profile. This could involve:

*   close liaison with the risk manager throughout the progress of the matter;
*   selecting the matter for an independent file review.

4.5.6 Risk recording and reporting

Risk must be considered at the start of, during the progress of and at the conclusion of a matter. The fact that a risk assessment has taken place must be recorded, for example, on a file summary sheet. It should be noted that, during the retainer, it is only necessary to record a risk if it has changed from the initial assessment.

A key element of risk control here is the necessity for the adviser to immediately inform the risk manager when:

- a new instruction has a high risk profile or an unusual element to it;
- there are any changes in the progress of a matter, for example, counsel's opinion casting doubt on advice already provided to the client;
- an end of matter review indicates the potential for a complaint or a claim.

The reporting of each of the above to the risk manager can be facilitated through the completion of a risk referral form.

A suggested format for a file summary sheet can be found at **Annex 4A**.

A suggested format for a risk referral form can be found at **Annex 4B**.

A flowchart highlighting the risk control actions to be taken throughout the progress of a matter can be found at **Annex 4C**.

> **Note:** Any material changes in the progress of a matter must be reported to the client immediately.

4.5.7 Mortgage fraud

Practices must designate a person with specific responsibility for mortgage fraud procedures and must review these procedures at least annually. This will reduce the risks of:

- fraudulent activity;
- exposure to disciplinary action and/or prosecution;
- reputational damage.

The practice should highlight the warning signs that personnel in the property department should be aware of and the steps they must take to notify the person responsible for mortgage fraud within the practice.

The Law Society produces a Practice Note on mortgage fraud which can be found at **www.lawsociety.org.uk/productsandservices/practicenotes/mortgagefraud.page**.

4.5.8 Key dates

A key date should be seen as any date which, if missed, could give rise to a claim against or a loss by your practice. Recording key dates both on the matter file and in a backup system will reduce the risk of them being overlooked.

It is essential that you have a system in place to monitor key dates to reduce the risk of a date being missed. Missing key dates continues to account for a large percentage of negligence claims against solicitors. Therefore it is vital that robust recording and monitoring arrangements are in place to which all personnel adhere.

4.5.9 Conflicts of interest

Practices must adopt a systematic approach to identifying and avoiding conflicts of interest, dealing with conflicts between the duties of confidentiality and disclosure, and maintaining client confidentiality.

Whereas conflicts may often arise at the outset of a matter, they could emerge at any stage. Advisers need to be alert to this and take necessary action should a conflict occur.

4.5.10 File checks

There is a requirement for those doing legal work to regularly check their files for inactivity (see 6.11 of Lexcel v4.1). This process reduces the risk of:

- client dissatisfaction and possible claims arising from unnecessary delays;
- client billing being overlooked.

There are a number of methods that practices can employ in order to conduct such checks. For example, a check on when time was last recorded on a matter or a trawl of the matter files to ensure that matters are progressing appropriately.

4.5.11 File reviews

Regular file reviews will reduce the risk of the errors and omissions that can occur during the life cycle of matters. In addition to those listed at **4.5.10**, such errors would include:

- risk assessments not being carried out;
- non-compliance with client care requirements;
- failure to record key dates.

File reviews are also extremely useful for identifying potential client complaints and possible indemnity claims and for setting remedial action in train at an early stage.

Note: The onus is on practices themselves to decide the number and frequency of file reviews. Generally, the factors to consider are:

- adviser experience;
- previous file reviews;
- workloads;
- risk profile of the matter; or
- practice area.

An important point to remember, however, is that the scope of file reviews must embrace all matter handlers, including senior managers.

File reviews should cover both procedural file management and substantive legal content. An approach that tends to work well in most practices is a focus on procedural compliance through file reviews, with the monitoring of substantive legal content taking place via caseload reviews and supervision.

It is not a requirement for file reviews to be undertaken by the designated supervisor. However, it is a requirement for the designated supervisor to monitor the data generated by file reviews.

A suggested format for a file review checklist can be found at **Annex 4D**.

In the event of a file review identifying errors or omissions:

- Remedial action should take place as soon as possible and, in any case, within 28 days.
- The reviewer must verify that the remedial action has taken place.

Details of any corrective actions taken must be recorded. A suggested format for a file review corrective action form can be found at **Annex 4E**.

4.6 Risk management action plan

It is good practice to compile a risk management action plan. This enables the following key information to be defined:

- the specific actions required to reduce levels of risk;
- the specific responsibilities for the management of identified risks;
- the target dates for the implementation of specific actions.

An example of a risk management action plan can be found at **Annex 4F**.

Annex 4A

File summary sheet

Client name		Date file opened	
Fee earner		Matter number	

Initial risk assessment

Risk rating: Low ☐   Medium ☐   High ☐   **Referred to risk manager** ☐

Procedure	Action	Date
Client objectives recorded		
Client identification verified		
Conflict of interest check conducted		
Case plan completed		
Method of funding established and cost-benefit analysis conducted		
Key dates recorded on file and in backup system		
Client engagement letter issued		
Procedure	**Action**	**Date**
Client notified of change in fee earner/supervisor		
Conflict of interest conducted		
Client updated on costs		
Client informed of adverse costs order		
Undertaking given		
Barrister or other service provider instructed		
Complaints procedure forwarded to client		

Interim risk assessment

Change in risk profile?   Yes ☐   No ☐   **Referred to risk manager** ☐

Procedure	Action	Date
Client notified of outcome		
Account to client for any outstanding money		
Original documents returned to client		
Original documents retained on behalf of client		
Client advised on storage and retrieval of papers		
Client advised of matter review process		
Archive		
Date to destroy		

Concluding risk assessment

Client objectives achieved?   Yes   ☐   No   ☐   **Referred to risk manager**   ☐

Annex 4B

Risk referral form

Client details	
Client name:	
Matter number:	
Stage of matter	
Please indicate the stage of the matter at which the risk has been identified.	
Start of matter	☐
During matter	☐
Conclusion of matter	☐
Reason for referral	
Please state rationale for referral to the risk manager:	
Signed:	
Print name:	
Date:	
Action	
The following action has been taken by the risk manager:	
Signed:	
Print name:	
Date:	

Annex 4C

Operational risk flowchart

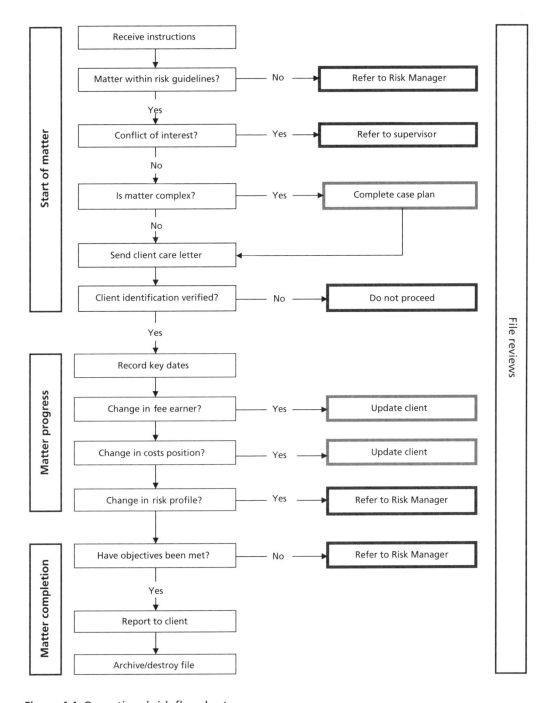

Figure 4.1 Operational risk flowchart

Annex 4D

File review checklist

Matter number		Fee earner	
Reviewer		Date	

Note: Procedures need to be addressed in a timely manner to be compliant

Procedure	Compliance		
	Yes	No	N/A
Start of matter			
Initial risk assessment conducted and recorded	☐	☐	☐
Client identification verified	☐	☐	☐
Conflict of interest check conducted	☐	☐	☐
Method of funding established and cost-benefit analysis conducted	☐	☐	☐
Key dates recorded on file and in backup system	☐	☐	☐
Client engagement letter issued	☐	☐	☐
Progress of matter			
Client updated on costs as appropriate	☐	☐	☐
Client updated on change of fee earner or supervisor	☐	☐	☐
Timely response made to client enquiries	☐	☐	☐
Risk manager informed of change in risk profile	☐	☐	☐
Client informed in event of adverse costs order	☐	☐	☐
Undertakings correctly discharged	☐	☐	☐
Barristers and expert witnesses, etc. engaged in line with procedures	☐	☐	☐
Complaints procedure followed	☐	☐	☐
Time recording	☐	☐	☐
Clients billed in accordance with agreed terms	☐	☐	☐
End of matter			
Client notified of outcome	☐	☐	☐
Client accounted to for any outstanding money	☐	☐	☐
Original documents returned to client	☐	☐	☐
Original documents retained on behalf of client	☐	☐	☐

Client advised on storage and retrieval of papers	☐	☐	☐
Client advised of matter review process	☐	☐	☐
Concluding risk assessment conducted	☐	☐	☐
File organisation	☐	☐	☐
Matter strategy and status apparent from file	☐	☐	☐
Documents stored in an orderly way	☐	☐	☐

Overall outcome: Compliant   ☐   Non-compliant   ☐

Note: If non-compliant please complete file review corrective action form

Comments

Copy placed on matter file   ☐   Copy to supervisor   ☐   Copy to risk manager   ☐

Annex 4E
File review corrective action form

Matter number:		File review date:	
Referred to:		Date:	

Please see attached file review checklist. The following non-compliances have been identified:

Please detail corrective action taken and return to the reviewer within 28 days of the file review date.

Signed:

Print name:

Date:

Please refer back to reviewer for corrective action to be verified

Verification
Corrective action form received on:

I confirm that the necessary remedial action has/has not been completed.

Signed:

Print name:

Date:

Copy placed on matter file   ☐   Copy to supervisor   ☐   Copy to risk manager   ☐

Annex 4F

Risk management action plan

Risk	Current level	Target level	Action	Responsibility	By when	Outcome
Ineffective performance measurement and review	High	Medium	Introduce formal file review procedure	Risk manager	30.4.10	Achieved
			Re-design client survey process	Client care manager	31.5.10	Achieved
			Formally analyse data relating to file reviews, complaints and claims	Risk manager	30.9.10	
			Introduce system of strategic performance reviews	Senior management team	30.9.10	
Inconsistent application of client identification procedure	High	Medium	Initiate update training on anti-money laundering procedures	Money laundering reporting officer	30.4.10	Achieved
			Introduce formal file review procedure	Risk manager	30.4.10	Achieved
Insufficiently robust data security systems	High	Medium	Deliver training in data protection and information management procedures	Training manager	31.5.10	WIP
			Upgrade IT security software	IT manager	30.6.10	Achieved
			Introduce periodic IT security audits	Risk manager	31.7.10	
Lack of structured system for allocation of work	High	Medium	Conduct monthly matter reviews with each fee earner	Supervisors	30.4.10	Achieved
			Deliver workshop on supervision procedures	Risk manager	31.5.10	Achieved
Insufficiently robust systems for vetting instructions	High	Medium	Define the type of work that falls within the practice's capability	Senior management team	30.4.10	Achieved
			Introduce procedure for considering and recording matter risk profiles	Risk manager	30.4.10	Achieved
			Brief all fee earners on new procedure	Risk manager	31.5.10	WIP

Risk	Current level	Target level	Action	Responsibility	By when	Outcome
Non-compliance with health and safety legislation	Medium	Low	Appointed person to undertake health and safety management training	Practice manager	30.6.10	Achieved
			Introduce system of risk assessments and audits	Practice manager	30.9.10	
Periodic instances of poor cash flow	Medium	Low	Brief fee earners on billing procedures	Cashier	30.4.10	Achieved
			Introduce system of interim billing	Finance manager	31.5.10	Achieved
			Introduce quarterly income and expenditure reviews	Finance manager	30.6.10	Achieved
Inconsistent compliance with rule 2	Medium	Low	Design standard client engagement letters	Client care manager	30.4.10	Achieved
			Introduce formal file review procedure	Risk manager	30.4.10	Achieved
Insufficient flow of new instructions	Medium	Low	Compile marketing plan	Senior management team	30.6.10	WIP
			Recruit business development manager	Practice manager	31.12.10	
Catastrophic event such as fire or flooding	Medium	Low	Compile business continuity plan	Risk manager	31.5.10	Achieved
			Conduct periodic tests to gauge effectiveness of plan	Risk manager	30.9.10	
			Upgrade buildings and contents insurance cover	Practice manager	31.7.10	

Dates reviewed: 14.7.10

5 Risk monitoring

5.1 Overview

You need to keep the risk management framework under continual review to ensure that it remains relevant and effective. The overall review process includes:

- ongoing monitoring – particularly for high risk activities;
- a strategic review at least annually;
- record keeping.

5.2 Ongoing monitoring

Ongoing risk monitoring ensures that risk identification and risk treatment processes are working and that any necessary remedial actions are taken at the earliest possible opportunity. For example, your practice should have:

- a process for monitoring key dates;
- a procedure for monitoring the data generated by file reviews;
- a procedure to monitor client satisfaction;
- a procedure for monitoring undertakings.

5.2.1 Key dates

Failure to comply with time limits is a significant cause of claims. As well as documenting key dates, you need processes for monitoring adherence to those dates.

5.2.2 File review data

The data generated by file reviews must be reviewed and monitored by the designated supervisor. The frequency with which monitoring takes place should be determined by the practice and, principally, it should be used to:

- identify trends;
- identify and initiate improvement actions;
- feed into a strategic level review of risk data.

Where file reviews are not routinely conducted by designated supervisors, they must ensure that they make themselves aware of the results of the reviews and take any necessary action.

The principal reasons for analysing data are to identify opportunities for improving quality and reducing risk. A key aspect of this is the identification of trends or patterns which may highlight the need to take remedial actions. Typically, these remedial actions could be a tightening of supervision procedures, a need for further staff training or a strengthening of communication.

A template risk data analysis form can be found at **Annex 5A**.

5.2.3   Client satisfaction

Practices must have a process to monitor client satisfaction. The method is not prescriptive – it can, for example, be done via structured surveys or through client review meetings. Whereas the minimum frequency with which monitoring should be carried out is annually, it is good practice to gather feedback on an ongoing basis. This type of approach enables the quality of client service to be measured and continually improved and reduces the risk of clients making complaints or taking their business elsewhere.

The data emanating from client feedback should also be analysed and reviewed as part of the strategic review of risk (see **5.3**).

5.2.4   Undertakings

There are significant risks associated with poor control of undertakings, such as financial loss and disciplinary action. Procedures must be in place, therefore, relating to the giving, monitoring and discharge of undertakings.

5.3   Strategic review

The effectiveness of risk management across a practice must be formally reviewed at least annually. This review process could focus on risk management specifically, or be done as part of a wider strategic review of all areas of practice management.

A strategic review of risk management should include:

- a review of the risk management policy;
- a review of the health and safety policy;
- a review and test of the business continuity plan;
- a review of mortgage fraud procedures;
- an analysis of risk assessment data relating to indemnity insurance claims, client complaints and file reviews;
- an analysis of risk assessment data relating to client feedback.

It is good practice to also utilise strategic risk reviews to:

- assess the performance of the practice against its risk management objectives;
- assess the overall performance of the practice in terms of its business objectives;

- measure progress against the risk management action plan;
- update the risk register.

> **Note:** Once your strategic risk review is completed, the information should be fed into your practice's wider strategic planning process. This will aid the completion of business and training plans. It may also be considered appropriate to report to relevant stakeholders such as staff, investors, bankers and insurers.

A suggested agenda for a strategic risk review can be found at **Annex 5B**.

An example of strategic risk review minutes can be found at **Annex 5C**.

In the event of a practice electing to have a full strategic review there is also a need to:

- review all practice management policies;
- review strategic plans such as marketing, business, ICT, recruitment and training;
- review financial data;
- review financial management processes;
- review billing processes;
- review procedures for handling financial transactions;
- review the office manual.

A strategic review matrix indicating which reviews should take place, and their frequency, can be found at **Annex 5D**.

5.4 Record keeping

Effective record keeping is an essential part of the risk monitoring process. The following must be recorded and retained centrally:

- office manual amendments;
- person specifications or job descriptions;
- recruitment interview notes;*
- file review records;
- standing terms of business with regular clients;
- client complaints;
- a list of barristers and experts.

Furthermore it is deemed good practice to keep central records in relation to:

- health and safety risk assessments;
- staff induction;
- staff training;
- undertakings.

In addition to the above lists, there could also be legal and regulatory requirements to keep some records. Money laundering reports and health and safety training records would be examples of these.

It is also advised that practices retain copies of risk registers as this will allow changes in risk profiles to be charted and may be of interest to insurers.

---

*Note: The Employment Practices Data Protection Code (Part 1) provides that interview notes should not be kept for longer than one year.

Annex 5A
Risk data analysis form

Review period:			

1. File reviews

Data	No.	%
File reviews conducted		
Files requiring corrective action		
Corrective action taken within 28 days		

Trend analysis

Record brief description of any trends, for example, errors linked to a particular procedure or a particular department.

2. Complaints

Data	No.	%
Matters opened		
Complaints received		

Trend analysis

Record brief description of any trends, for example, complaints linked to a type of matter or a particular department.

3. Indemnity claims	
Data	**No.**
Number of indemnity claims received	

Trend analysis

Record brief description of any trends, for example, claims linked to a type of matter or a particular time period.

4. Remedial action
Record brief description of any remedial actions identified to address issues arising from risk data analysis.

Signed: **Name:**   **Date:**

Annex 5B
Strategic risk review agenda

1   Summary of business performance

- Review the overall performance of the practice against its main business objectives.

2   Risk management action plan

- Review progress against plan and update outcomes.

3   Risk assessment data

- Analyse and review performance and trends relating to:

  - Indemnity claims
  - Client complaints
  - File review data
  - Client satisfaction surveys

4   Health and safety policy

- Review policy and verify its effectiveness.

5   Business continuity plan

- Review content of plan.
- Review testing procedures.

6   Mortgage fraud procedures

- Review procedures and verify their effectiveness.

7   Risk register

- Conduct risk assessment.
- Update register.

8   Risk management policy

- Review policy and verify its effectiveness.

9   AOB

[Include items]

Annex 5C
Strategic risk review minutes and action points

Date: [*insert date*]

In attendance: [*name of attendees*]

1   Business performance

An overview of performance results was distributed and discussed.

2   Risk management action plan

The plan was formally reviewed and updated.

3   Risk assessment data

A client survey analysis report was distributed among the team. Whereas there were consistently high ratings for the quality of legal advice, ratings were comparatively low in respect of promptness of replies and the quality of the reception service.

Notwithstanding client feedback on promptness of replies, it was agreed that statistics relating to complaints and claims were still within acceptable parameters.

File review data was distributed among the team. Whereas overall results were positive, concerns were raised over the number of cases where staff had not taken steps to verify client identity.

Action required and owner

- Specific service levels to be introduced for speed of response to client enquiries. [*Initials*]
- Reception staff to undertake additional training in client care. [*Initials*]
- All staff to attend money laundering briefings. [*Initials*]

4   Health and safety policy

The policy was reviewed and signed off – no updates required.

5   Business continuity plan

The content of the business continuity plan was formally reviewed. It was acknowledged that it was a thorough document addressing all potential risks. However, it was felt not all staff may be aware of emergency procedures.

Action required and owner

Questionnaire to be distributed to test staff understanding of business continuity strategy. [*Initials*]

6 Mortgage fraud procedures

Concern was raised over implementation of procedures relating to client identification checking.

Action required

See item 3.

7 Risk register

A thorough analysis of strategic, operational and regulatory risk was conducted. Levels of risk were formally estimated and agreed.

Action required and owner

Risk register to be updated and communicated to all staff. [*Initials*]

8 Risk management policy

It was felt that the policy may need to be updated in the light of outcomes-focused regulation.

Action required and owner

Requirements of outcomes-focused regulation to be researched and policy updated as required. [*Initials*]

9 AOB

- Compliance with rule 5 of the Solicitors' Code of Conduct was formally reviewed.
- Action is currently underway to update the office manual in line with the revised requirements of Lexcel.
- It was felt that insufficient action took place to forecast potential recruitment needs.

Action required and owner

- Office manual to be checked for compliance prior to Lexcel assessment. [*Initials*]
- Anticipated recruitment needs to be included in the business plan. [*Initials*]

Annex 5D
Strategic risk review matrix

The chart below provides guidance on the recommended minimum frequency with which reviews must be conducted.

Category	Subject	Lexcel reference	Frequency		
			Quarterly	Biannually	Annually
Plans	Marketing and business plan	2.1		•	
	Business continuity plan	2.3			•
	ICT plan	2.4			•
	Recruitment plan	5.1			•
	Training and development plan	5.2			•
Policies	Risk management policy	1.2			•
	Quality policy	1.3			•
	Equality and diversity policy	1.4			•
	Health and safety policy	1.5			•
	Community and social responsibility policy	1.6			•
	Information management policy	4.1			•
	E-mail policy	4.2			•
	Website management policy	4.3			•
	Internet access policy	4.4			•
	Training and development policy	5.7			•
	Client care policy	7.1			•
Financial data	Income and expenditure	3.2	•		
	Cash flow	3.2	•		
	Billing procedures	3.4			•
	Financial transactions	3.5			•
Risk data	Indemnity claims data	6.14			•
	Client complaints data	6.14			•
	File review data	6.14			•
	Client satisfaction data	7.6			•
Other	Services	2.2		•	
	Office manual	4.6			•
	Mortgage fraud procedures	6.5			•

6 Risk management culture

6.1 Overview

As well as having structured risk management processes in place, you need to create the right environment for risk management to be effective. First of all, it is important to achieve the right balance in terms of risk management activity. On the one hand, processes and procedures need to be robust; on the other, too obsessive an approach can be counter-productive. As a general rule, the approach to risk should:

- be proportionate, consistent and targeted;
- not inhibit your practice's capability to be competitive and deliver high quality client care;
- not compromise mutual trust and team work;
- not seek to apportion blame.

Culture is sometimes described as 'the way things are done around here' and, as such, can encompass many different elements. In developing a risk management culture, it is best to focus on:

- leadership;
- responsibility;
- continuous learning.

6.2 Leadership

The quality of leadership can have a huge bearing on the success or failure of risk management in a practice. Organisations that operate effective risk management tend to have senior managers displaying the following leadership characteristics:

- commitment and role modelling;
- sound decision making;
- effective engagement of people.

6.2.1 Commitment and role modelling

Strong commitment can be demonstrated by allocating sufficient resources to risk management and by actively participating in the process. People in key risk management positions, such as supervisors, must be given the time and support needed to fulfil their duties. Also, senior managers should act as role models by consistently complying with policies, processes and procedures. This is particularly true with regard to file reviews where a lack of senior management 'buy-in' will inevitably weaken the credibility and the integrity of the process.

6.2.2 Decision making

Having excellent risk identification processes is, in itself, not enough. Arguably, some of the high street banks ran into trouble not through a lack of awareness of their risks but, rather, poor decision making based on the information they had at their disposal.

The need for decision making mainly comes into play in respect of strategic risks that have a potential upside as well as a downside. In the context of a legal practice these could be the risks associated with, for example, an office relocation. The key here is to make fully informed decisions by considering all the possible consequences. A good question to ask when making these decisions is 'What if?'

For example:

- What if the economy contracts and there is downward pressure on fee income?
- What if interest rates increase significantly?

6.2.3 People engagement

In any organisation it makes sound business sense to harness and utilise the talents of all members of the workforce. An effective risk management culture can be developed by:

- encouraging all staff to identify and report risks;
- communicating risk management plans;
- acknowledging and recognising good risk management practice;
- communicating risk management performance;
- encouraging staff to suggest ideas for improvement (see **Annex 6A**).

6.3 Responsibility

There must be clearly defined lines of risk management responsibility throughout each practice area and all support functions. One designated person must have overall responsibility for risk management – this person is known as the risk manager. The risk manager should be a person with sufficient seniority and influence to ensure that risk management is accorded appropriate importance. Other key roles within the sphere of risk management include:

- money laundering reporting officer (MLRO);*
- complaints manager;
- supervisors.

It should be noted that one individual may occupy more than one or all of these roles – this is often the case in smaller practices.

In order to ensure consistency and rigour, it is good practice to define the purpose and responsibilities of each of the above roles within written role definitions. Precedent role definitions are included as **Annex 6B**.

In a more general sense, everyone in the practice should take responsibility for risk management processes. Therefore, it is good practice to include risk-related responsibilities in everyone's role definition. For example, the following requirements could be inserted into the role definitions of all employees:

- notify the risk manager in the event of a new instruction having a high risk profile;
- report any suspicion of money laundering or mortgage fraud to the MLRO;
- inform the risk manager if there are any unusual circumstances in the progress of a matter;
- notify the risk manager in the event of a concluding risk assessment highlighting the possibility of a claim or a complaint.

---

*Note: The MLRO role could be combined with responsibility for mortgage fraud procedures.

6.4 Continuous learning

Training and development has an enormous effect on the full spectrum of the risk management process. As a general principle, employees should be given the training necessary to equip them with the knowledge and skills required to discharge their risk management responsibilities effectively. Specifically, for Lexcel, there are mandatory requirements to ensure that training has taken place with regard to:

- information management;
- induction;
- supervision and management.

In addition, there are regulatory requirements to provide training in relation to, for example:

- health and safety;
- anti-money laundering procedures;
- continuing professional development.

It is particularly important that personnel are competent to carry out their specific responsibilities relating to risk management. For roles such as risk manager, MLRO, complaints manager, health and safety manager and supervisor this may necessitate specialised training. For personnel generally, it may be appropriate to update their knowledge through team meetings or risk briefings.

Risk management is a dynamic concept in the sense that the factors that cause risk are not constant. It is vital, therefore, that risk training is not a one-off event – it must be updated to keep pace with any changes that occur.

A template induction checklist can be found at **Annex 6C.**

Annex 6A
Staff suggestion form

Business management
Improvement suggestions could relate to areas such as business strategy, finance, ICT, library services or general office procedures.
My improvement suggestion is:

Client management
Improvement suggestions could relate to areas such as marketing, service levels, file and case management or use of counsel.
My improvement suggestion is:

People management
Improvement suggestions could relate to areas such as recruitment, induction, appraisals, communication, training and development or staff reward and recognition.
My improvement suggestion is:

Risk management
Improvement suggestions could relate to areas such as supervision, the vetting process, anti-money laundering procedures, file reviews or staff safety.
My improvement suggestion is:

Name:
Date:

Annex 6B
Role definitions

Job title: Risk Manager

Key purpose

To identify and manage all strategic, operational and regulatory risks that may arise within the practice.

Key responsibilities

- Ensure that the practice's risk management policy and risk register are current and robust.
- Ensure that the practice is compliant with all professional rules.
- Liaise with the senior management team to ensure that the practice has effective corporate governance procedures in place.
- Ensure that risk management is an integral part of the strategic planning process.
- Oversee the identification and treatment of the operational risks associated with the day-to-day management of the practice.
- Liaise with the Quality Manager to ensure that the office manual is fully compliant with practice procedures.
- Maintain a list of work that the practice will and will not undertake.
- Maintain a list of generic risks and causes of claims.
- Make decisions on the acceptance of instructions that have a higher risk profile than the norm within the practice.
- Ensure that there are robust systems relating to the security and confidentiality of all data, both electronic and hard copy, held by the practice.
- Ensure that there are robust systems in place for the supervision of staff and the supervision of client matters.
- Ensure that file reviews are conducted in line with documented procedures.
- Ensure that there is analysis (at least annually) of risk data relating to claims, complaints and file reviews.
- Ensure that there is adequate risk management training for all staff, particularly in relation to money laundering, data protection and information management.
- Ensure that there are appropriate systems in place for the reporting of risks.
- Ensure that the practice has procedures in place to enable it to exercise its duty of care with regard to the health, safety and welfare of employees and visitors.
- Ensure that the practice has adequate and current indemnity insurance.
- Ensure that the practice has a robust strategy for business recovery and continuity in the light of catastrophic events.
- Act as a role model by visibly adhering to the practice's risk management policy and procedures.

Job title: Complaints Manager

Key purpose

To ensure that the practice has effective complaints management procedures.

Key responsibilities

- Promote a culture of high quality client care and effective complaints management.
- Liaise with the Quality Manager and the Risk Manager to ensure that there is compliance with the relevant professional rules.
- Ensure that information on how and where to complain is well publicised to clients.
- Ensure that there are adequate resources allocated to client care and complaints management.
- Oversee processes for receiving, recording, investigating and responding to complaints.
- Ensure that all complaints are handled promptly, fairly and effectively.
- Ensure that complaints are dealt with in accordance with the practice's procedures.
- Ensure that all staff are aware of client care policy and standards.
- Liaise with the Training Partner to ensure that all staff have the knowledge and skills to provide high quality client care and effective complaints management.
- Record all complaints on the central complaints register.
- Liaise with the Quality Manager to ensure that the office manual is fully compliant with professional rules.
- Keep abreast of best practice in complaints avoidance and complaints resolution.
- Liaise with the Legal Ombudsman where appropriate.
- Act as a role model by visibly adhering to the practice's client care policy and by exercising good complaints management behaviour.
- Seek continuous improvement by providing the Risk Manager with qualitative feedback and statistical results data arising from complaints.

Job title: Money Laundering Reporting Officer

Key purpose

To ensure that the practice complies with all legislation relating to the prevention of money laundering, terrorist financing and mortgage fraud.

Key responsibilities

- Create the culture and values that will enable the practice to implement successful procedures for the prevention of money laundering, terrorist financing and mortgage fraud.

- Periodically assess the money laundering and mortgage fraud risk levels particular to the practice, and implement reasonable and considered controls to minimise those risks.
- Establish and maintain appropriate and risk-sensitive policies and procedures relating to client identification and verification, client due diligence, reporting, record keeping and monitoring.
- Liaise with the Quality Manager to ensure that the anti-money laundering and mortgage fraud procedures in the office manual are appropriate and up to date.
- Ensure that all employees are regularly trained in anti-money laundering procedures at a level appropriate to their role.
- Conduct periodic file reviews to ensure that staff are consistently exercising all due diligence procedures.
- Monitor and evaluate the anti-money laundering policy on an ongoing basis.
- Formally review the anti-money laundering policy in the event of updates to legislation and, in any case, on an annual basis.
- Act as a role model by visibly adhering to the practice's anti-money laundering policy and mortgage fraud procedures.
- Seek continuous improvement by providing the Risk Manager with qualitative feedback and statistical results data arising from file reviews.

Job title: Supervisor

Key purpose

The identification, treatment and monitoring of the operational risks associated with the day-to-day management of the practice.

Key responsibilities

- Make decisions on the acceptance of instructions that have a higher risk profile than the norm within the practice.
- Liaise with the Risk Manager to ensure that generic risk lists are kept up to date.
- Ensure that team members are kept informed of specific and generic risks.
- Ensure that there are robust systems in place for the monitoring of key dates.
- Check incoming and outgoing correspondence, including letters, e-mails and faxes as prescribed by the procedures in the office manual.
- Ensure that there are appropriate team communication structures in place.
- Conduct periodic reviews of matters to ensure good financial controls and appropriate allocation of workloads.
- Ensure that team members are allocated workloads within their capacity and capability.
- Ensure that file reviews are conducted in line with documented procedures.
- Review and monitor the data generated by file reviews.
- Ensure that there is consistent implementation of case management procedures relating to the assessment and recording of operational risks.

- Ensure that there are robust systems relating to the security and confidentiality of all data, both electronic and hard copy, held by the practice.
- Act as a role model by visibly adhering to the practice's risk management policies and procedures.
- Seek continuous improvement by providing the Risk Manager with qualitative feedback and statistical results data arising from the monitoring of file reviews.

Note: This role definition only covers those aspects of supervision directly relating to risk management. Other aspects of the supervisory role, such as people management, will need to be added.

Annex 6C
Induction checklist

Name of employee	
Job title	
Start date	

Action	Name of inductor	Initials	Date
Module 1: Terms and conditions			
P45 received			
Personal details recorded			
Salary and expenses			
Office hours (flexitime/overtime)			
Holiday entitlement and procedure			
Absence – notification procedure			
Sick pay entitlement			
Probationary period			
Periods of notice/temporary contracts			
Contract of employment issued			
Module 2: Health and safety			
Health and safety policy			
Tour of workplace			
Fire procedures			
Safety precautions			
Hazards reporting			
Accident procedures			
Housekeeping			
First aid procedures			
Personal security			
Office security			
Module 3: About the practice			
History of the practice			
Mission, vision and values			
Business objectives			
Introduction to colleagues			

Action	Name of inductor	Initials	Date
Module 4: Policies, procedures and role definition			
Client care policy			
Risk management policy			
Anti-money laundering policy			
Quality policy			
Equality and diversity policy			
Data protection policy			
E-mail policy			
Information management policy			
Other policies			
Business continuity			
Quality procedures manual			
File management procedures			
Accounts procedures			
IT systems			
Stationery/office equipment			
Secretarial arrangements			
Communication processes			
Job description/role definition			
Module 5: Training and development			
Training and development policy/CPD			
Money laundering			
Information management			
Data protection			
Analysis of initial training needs			
Appraisals			
Library and information services			

I confirm that this employee has successfully completed all elements of the induction programme.
Name   Position
Signature   Date
I confirm that I have received and understood the information itemised above.
Name   Position
Signature   Date

7 SWOT and PEST analyses

7.1 Overview

SWOT and PEST analyses are tried and tested techniques that can be utilised for risk management. Collectively, they provide a framework for identifying both the current issues affecting a practice and any future circumstances that could prevail.

7.2 SWOT analysis

SWOT is an acronym referring to:

- Strengths
- Weaknesses
- Opportunities
- Threats

The analysis of strengths and weaknesses relates to the present and, as can be seen, focuses on internal factors within a practice. The analysis of opportunities and threats, on the other hand, relates to external influences and should be based on the future as well as the present.

A SWOT analysis is usually presented in the form of a matrix as depicted below:

Internal factors	Strengths	Weaknesses
	Highly motivated staff	Outdated IT systems
	Marketing strategy	Insufficient investment in management training
	High levels of technical competence among fee earners	Poor cash flow
	Financial reserves	High overheads
	Reputation	Ineffective performance measurement and review
External factors	**Opportunities**	**Threats**
	Alternative business structures	Alternative business structures
	Aging population	Flat housing market
	Wills and probate work	Competition from other practices
	Acquisition or merger	E-law
	Re-mortgage and repossession work	Bank lending restrictions
	Outcomes-focused regulation	Public sector funding cuts

A template SWOT matrix can be found at **Annex 7A.**

7.3 PEST analysis

A PEST analysis complements a SWOT analysis in that it provides a framework for identifying potential opportunities and threats. The acronym refers to:

- Political
- Economic
- Social
- Technological

When assessing opportunities and threats it is necessary to make some assumptions. This is often the most difficult aspect of the risk assessment process because the answers are often not certain and many influences are beyond the control of a practice.

In essence, a PEST analysis is based on identifying the events that could take place in the political, economic, social and technological spheres. Examples of this are as follows.

7.3.1 Political

Typical considerations could include the potential effect on a practice that could be brought about by political events such as:

- change of government;
- legislative change;
- regulatory change.

7.3.2 Economic

Typical considerations could include the potential effect on a practice that could be brought about by economic factors such as:

- interest rates;
- inflation;
- unemployment.

7.3.3 Social

Typical considerations could include the potential effect on a practice that could be brought about by social factors such as:

- a change in population levels;
- a change in the demographic profile of the area.

7.3.4 Technological

Typical considerations could include the potential effect on a practice that could be brought about by technological change such as:

* advancements in ICT.

7.4 The process

Ordinarily, a SWOT and PEST exercise would be done in a management team meeting or a specific planning event. It could also be carried out at team level, for example, within a particular department.

The process would usually involve drawing a SWOT matrix on a flip chart and then carrying out a brainstorming exercise among the group. In relation to strengths and weaknesses the two key questions to ask are:

* What are we good at?
* Where do we need to improve?

With regard to opportunities and threats the questions to ask should be along the lines of:

* What if ...?
* What would be the implications of ...?
* What would happen in the event of ...?

Once the exercise is complete, your identified weaknesses and threats will largely determine the content of your risk register and may also influence your training plan.

Your strengths and opportunities, on the other hand can be used to inform the content of your marketing and business plan.

Note: This process may also be referred to as a 'PESTLE' analysis by including the additional categories 'legal' and 'environmental'. However, the principle of utilising the process as a framework for identifying opportunities and threats remains the same.

Annex 7A
SWOT analysis matrix

Internal factors	Strengths	Weaknesses
External factors	Opportunities	Threats

8 Risk mapping

8.1 Numerical index version

Risk mapping allows a specific level to be allocated to different areas of risk. For example, you may have highlighted the following risks as part of the identification process:

A   Inconsistent application of procedure for verifying client identity
B   Poor cash flow due to inconsistent approach to billing
C   Severe flooding
D   Loss of photocopying facilities

The next step is to consider the likelihood and the impact of each risk and simply plot each outcome on the risk map as follows:

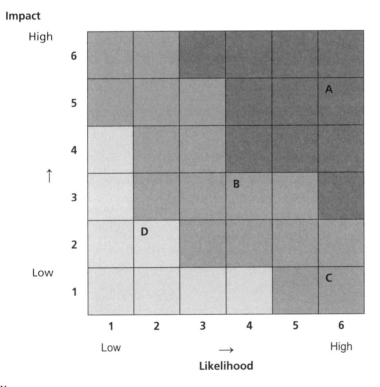

Key

1–4	Low risk
5–15	Medium risk
16–36	High risk

Figure 8.1 Risk map 1

57

The risk index is calculated by multiplying the likelihood coefficient by the impact coefficient. The risk rating is then gauged as follows:

Reference	Description	Level			
		Likelihood	Impact	Index	Rating
A	Inconsistent verification of client identity	5	6	30	High
B	Poor cash flow	3	4	12	Medium
C	Severe flooding	1	6	6	Medium
D	Loss of photocopying facilities	2	2	4	Low

Once the levels of all your main risks have been ascertained you can then transfer the information on to your risk register (see **Annex 3B**).

Low likelihood/low impact risks may be defined as acceptable and may not, therefore, require specific control measures. Conversely, those risks designated high likelihood/high impact will be given top prioritisation as part of the risk treatment process.

A template numerical index risk map can be found at **Annex 8A**.

8.2 Four box matrix

Some practices may wish to utilise a simplified four box version of the risk map. This option is not numerically based but can still be an effective means of identifying varying levels of risk.

As with the numerical index version it is simply a case of plotting the likelihood and the impact of each risk on the risk map as follows:

Key

Box 1	Low likelihood/Low impact
Box 2	Low likelihood/High impact
Box 3	High likelihood/Low impact
Box 4	High likelihood/High impact

Reference	Description	Probability	Impact	Rating
A	Inconsistent verification of client identity	High	High	High
B	Poor cash flow	High	Low	Medium
C	Severe flooding	Low	High	Medium
D	Loss of photocopying facilities	Low	Low	Low

Once the levels of all your main risks have been ascertained you can then transfer the information on to your risk register (see **Annex 3A**).

A template four box matrix risk map can be found at **Annex 8B**.

Annex 8A

Risk map 1

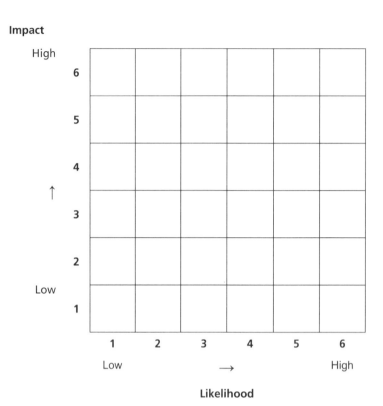

Impact

Likelihood

Annex 8B
Risk map 2

High	Box 3: Medium risk	Box 4: High risk
Impact	Box 1: Low risk	Box 2: Medium risk
Low		
	Low	**Likelihood** High

9 Health and safety

9.1 Legal responsibility

All employers have a legal responsibility to protect the health and safety of their staff and other people, such as clients and members of the public, who may be affected by their work.

In general, employers must:

- make the workplace safe and eliminate or control risks to health;
- ensure that plant and machinery are safe and that safe systems of work are set and followed;
- ensure that articles and substances are moved, stored and used safely;
- provide adequate welfare facilities;
- give workers the information, instruction, training and supervision necessary for their health and safety;
- consult workers on health and safety matters.

9.2 Requirements

9.2.1 Employers' Liability Compulsory Insurance

An Employers' Liability Compulsory Insurance certificate must be displayed where staff can easily read it.

9.2.2 Competent person

You must appoint someone competent to help your practice meet its health and safety duties. This could be an employee or an external consultant.

9.2.3 Health and safety policy

You must have a policy setting out the arrangements for managing health and safety in your practice. If your practice has five or more employees the policy must be in written format.

The details of a full health and safety policy will vary from practice to practice. A suggested format for an overarching health and safety policy can be found at **Annex 9A**.

9.2.4 Risk assessment

You must carry out risk assessments to decide what could harm people and what precautions need to be taken. You must act on the findings of your risk assessments by putting sensible controls in place to prevent accidents and ill health and making sure they are followed.

9.2.5 Welfare facilities

You must provide a safe and healthy environment for all your employees. This includes toilets, washing facilities and drinking water, and appropriate lighting and temperature.

9.2.6 Training and supervision

You must train your employees and contractors to work safely, and clearly instruct them in their duties. Health and safety training should take place during working hours and must not be paid for by employees. You also need to make sure that new, inexperienced or young employees are supervised.

9.2.7 Consultation

Workers must be consulted on their health and safety. This can be done with each employee individually or through health and safety representatives.

9.2.8 Health and safety law poster

You must display the health and safety law poster or, alternatively, provide workers with a leaflet.

9.2.9 RIDDOR

The Reporting of Injuries, Diseases and Dangerous Occurrences Regulations 1995 require you to report work-related accidents, diseases and near-miss incidents. Note that you are required to know how to report, even if you never need to.

> **Note:** The above information only represents an overview – for further detailed information, practices should consult with a health and safety specialist or contact the Health and Safety Executive.

Annex 9A
Health and safety policy

Commitment

[*Name of practice*] is committed to ensuring the safety of its employees, clients and anyone else affected by its business activities. The practice recognises its legal duties and will provide a safe working environment, safe work equipment and safe methods of work.

Scope

The scope of this policy embraces all permanent and temporary employees as well as visitors to the practice's premises.

Approach

The practice has set out the following strategy in relation to health and safety:

- to provide adequate control of the health and safety risks arising from work activities;
- to consult with our employees on matters affecting their health and safety;
- to provide and maintain safe equipment;
- to ensure safe handling and use of substances;
- to provide information, instruction and supervision for employees;
- to ensure that all employees are competent to do their tasks, and given adequate training;
- to prevent accidents and cases of work-related ill health;
- to maintain safe and healthy working conditions.

Responsibilities

Health and Safety Manager

The person with overall responsibility for health and safety in the practice is [*name of person*].

Senior management team

Section 2(1) of the Health and Safety at Work etc. Act 1974 provides that: 'It shall be the duty of every employer to ensure, so far as is reasonably practicable, the health, safety and welfare at work of all his employees.'

Staff

Section 7 of the Act requires employees to take reasonable care for the health and safety of themselves and other persons and to co-operate with their employer so far as is necessary to enable statutory requirements to be complied with.

Review

In order to ensure that it remains fit for purpose, this policy will be formally reviewed at least annually by the senior management team. This review process will also serve as a means of continually improving the practice's approach to risk management.

Signed:

[*Name*], Health and Safety Manager

Date:

10 Glossary

Risk	The combination of the likelihood of an event and its consequences
Risk assessment	A combination of the identification and evaluation of risks
Risk evaluation	The process for determining the level or severity of risks
Risk identification	The process of finding and recognising risks
Risk management action plan	A document setting out the key actions needed to manage the risks identified in the risk register
Risk management policy	Statement of the overall approach to risk management
Risk management framework	The structure of, and approach to, risk management including both process and culture
Risk manager	The designated person with overall responsibility for risk management in the practice
Risk monitoring	Continual review of risk management processes to determine effectiveness, key outcomes and opportunities for improvement
Risk register	A list of the main risks, their potential consequences and their respective levels
Risk treatment	Controlling risks through measures to accept, avoid, transfer or reduce